GETTING TO HEAVEN

(AND OTHER MIRACLES)

poems by

Gary Stein

Finishing Line Press
Georgetown, Kentucky

GETTING TO HEAVEN

(AND OTHER MIRACLES)

Copyright © 2023 by Gary Stein
ISBN 979-8-88838-143-4 First Edition
All rights reserved under International and Pan-American Copyright Conventions. No part of this book may be reproduced in any manner whatsoever without written permission from the publisher, except in the case of brief quotations embodied in critical articles and reviews.

ACKNOWLEDGMENTS

The following poems first appeared elsewhere, although some in slightly different form.

America: "Crossing El Rio San Pedro, Jonotla, Mexico"
Asheville Poetry Review: "Why Worms Rise to Rain"
Commonweal: "A Bough Falls" and "Flight"
The Atlanta Review: "While Viewing Renoir's Luncheon of the Boating Party"
Gargoyle: "Teegarden's Star" and "The Stuttering Anesthesiologist"
JAMA: "Why My Wife Should Let Me Have A Dog," and "Why The Dying Need Wills"
Speckled Trout Review: "Note to My Father As I Near the Age of His Death" (online)

Other poems appeared elsewhere including "In the Country, Deer" in my full length book, *Touring the Shadow Factory* and "Why the Dying Need Wills."

Special thanks to my wife, Cathy Henderson, the astute first reader of all these poems, and to my sons Jesse and Eliot, and grandson, Oliver Sebastián Lopez Stein, whose lives have enriched my poetry.

Publisher: Leah Huete de Maines
Editor: Christen Kincaid
Cover Art: Susan Makov
Author Photo: Cathy Henderson
Cover Design: Elizabeth Maines McCleavy

Order online: www.finishinglinepress.com
also available on amazon.com

Author inquiries and mail orders:
Finishing Line Press
PO Box 1626
Georgetown, Kentucky 40324
USA

Table of Contents

I. GETTING TO HEAVEN

A Bough Falls 1
Teegarden's Star 3
The Loneliness of Adam 4
Why Jesus Was So Good Picking Up Chicks 5
Flight 6
The Germ Of Faith 7
Why My Wife Should Let Me Have a Dog 8
Visiting Lori at Sibley Hospital 10
Joy in Heaven on the Return of the Egg That Was Lost 11
Lunchtime Apparition on Connecticut Avenue 12
The Stuttering Anesthesiologist 13
The Night My Glasses Fell into The Toilet Bowl of Clean Water 14

II: OTHER MIRACLES

Crossing El Rio San Pedro, Jonotla, Mexico 17
Note To My Father As I Near the Age of His Death 18
Haunted 20
Gross Anatomy: Georgetown Mini-Medical School 21
Why the Dying Need Wills 22
While Viewing Renoir's Luncheon of the Boating Party 23
Transport By GPS 24
In the Country, Deer 25
Why Worms Rise to Rain 26
Blind Harold 27
Advent 28
Discovery of The New World 29

I. GETTING TO HEAVEN

A BOUGH FALLS

Cut loose, betrayed by air it lands
like a lost gift on silent
indifferent earth until found

by a man of faith in an afterlife,
perhaps a priest in his black cassock
who later in a lonely rectory marries

imperfect oak to bundled kindling.
His match, a splinter of grace,
sparks petals of persistent light

into bloom and spreads healing
heat while wood whispers
like an angel in the quiet night.

Isn't fire just another prayer offered
to cure the darkness in time?
But every clock winds down

and wood turns to ash, and air
in the chimney chokes
on its smoke. The priest believes

that only when a soul is freed
from its body, like vapor
from the charred log, will it rise.

TEEGARDEN'S STAR

It's a long commute from Annapolis to the Goddard Space Center.
You can't afford to gaze at the eternity overhead.
Even an astrophysicist must focus on the concrete canyons
and blinking lights—the small glass stars on earthly cars.

Fifteen miles away I can't find my damn glasses again.
Not on the nightstand, or in the blue bowl on the marble table
in the foyer where memory placed them, and I don't know
if this is Alzheimer's first kiss on my bald head, the beginning
of the end, and whether I should call in sick again or call a cab
and go to work to provide a lesson in courage for the others.

Meanwhile, you survive the drive and, without even a dime store
telescope or fancy nuclear charged satellite equipped with
x-ray projectors, you discover a rare dwarf brown star
undetected although she hung in the universe
for billions of years, just waiting for this date
with you, and like a virgin bride she takes your name,
Teegarden's Star. Delicacy prevents me from asking
about the wild celebration that night.

Everyone knows a light year is a measure of the miles
light travels in one year: 10 to the 12th power times
5.8786625. But your star is more than 12 times further away
than that, a number streaking beyond the outer limits
of my earth-bound calculator. And I once thought my wife
a red-head from distant Richmond was a rare find.

And I haven't found God yet either. Perhaps He's waiting for us
just a few light years beyond your star. And if He's there,
I'm sure He's proud of you for discovering another dwarf star,
drifting unappreciated and lonely for so long, and God must think
I'm a fool for losing those glasses again, in a tiny house,

so insignificant in the cosmos, and for making light of the light
you've shown on the vast interstellar universe, and maybe
He's so pissed off at me, that Alzheimer's is His judgment
and not merely my momentary lapse in focus like when I wore
a brown shoe and a black shoe to that important meeting.

So if you're such a hotshot explorer, how about finding my glasses?
And if that task is too mundane, not elevated enough for a
goddamn Ph.D. from M.I.T. with his own star, then God may be
out there sitting in his heavenly rocking chair, patiently waiting
(just as we have waited for Him), for a scientist like you
with a distinguished beard, much like His, and on His lap
He may be holding your celestial Nobel Prize or
if you're a Muslim, waiting to turn you loose with 42
more virgin stars. And maybe He'll offer you a cold beer
before asking, "What took you so long to find me?"

THE LONELINESS OF ADAM

I won't forget the smells: bougainvillea, roses, jasmine.
Sure, Eden was swell and Eve sweet, well worth the rib
although I never saw Monroe or Hawaii.
Ominous nights: blinking stars were God's spying eyes,
the terrible silence—wordless world, God
everywhere and nowhere. His breath ruffled grass,
just cool air in my hair. He blew us off the garden
like nothing but seeds, rootless, aliens on earth.

Sure, you may say I was lucky—first person, father
of all mankind, Bible star.

But no one to mentor me, no guys to share a beer,
shoot the breeze, bond, strut my stuff.
Nothing to do but multiply, multiply, multiply.

WHY JESUS WAS SO GOOD PICKING UP CHICKS

We used to hang in school.
I know what I saw. His thing was this:
appearing out of nowhere, all ponytail
and cool sandals, sidling up,
circling the flock. Let loose
that piercing look, focus
on the wide hip, hair that would not curl,
heavy nose or eye that failed to track
quite quick enough—the flaw she hated most,
that kept her home—why she skipped
the pom-pom squad or never pledged.

He'd whisper in her ear.
I love full hips, your Semite nose. You know
I'm a Jew, like you.
I'd go blind to have that lovely lazy eye
wash me in its blue. I love straight hair,
the thing that makes you
you of all the world, makes you shy
even though you're hot, doubt even when I don't,
Your weakness is your strength. It's what I love.
It's who you are and all I want. Because
perfection is a perfect bore.

Who wouldn't fall for that,
drop her books, follow to his car
straight away.
Do anything he asked.

FLIGHT

When the small boy
in the red propeller beanie
walked across our feet
and out the pew

in the middle of Mass,
we all turned away
from our priest to watch
the child push the big oak door.

Then he leaned
into a strong Sabbath wind
having chosen
a quicker way to heaven.

THE GERM OF FAITH

One day the bishop came to class in his infinite hat
and flaunted down each aisle, tendering
his ring to our obedient, pursed lips.

Buried in the ring, a speck of bone under glass,
mortal remains of a saint whose name alone
erased a cancer. *A first-class relic*, said Sister
as she trailed His Eminence with a white cloth
to rub away our moist reverence.

And was the ring that housed the holy bone
a relic too, though second class,
yet worthy of respect? And then our lips,
third class? And the rag that buffed the ring,
the hand that rubbed the rag,
the robe that touched the hand?

A hundred ranks of holiness pull us through
each day to the dreamy rim of heaven.

WHY MY WIFE SHOULD LET ME HAVE A DOG

If I had a dog his soft fur would not foliate
the sofa or trigger asthma attacks
in my dear wife, ending with a hospital trip,
an adrenaline shot and those inhaler tubes
littering the house.

His rich brown eyes will convey profound
intelligence and sensitivity to the subtlest
shifts in my mood. Those eyes will never
get infected and fill with viscous yellow pus
we must wipe with Q-Tips and cure with
sticky ointment, awkward for us both.

My dog will lie by my feet while I read
the Sunday Times he fetched from the lawn
and delivered dry from his slobber-free
mouth, and he'll wait for his walk
until I complete the crossword.

And when we walk he'll heel until I hurl
a tennis ball. Watch him streak across
the grassy field, catch it on first bounce
and, with gleeful tail, surrender the prize to me
for another go. He will never drop dead
birds or vermin on the front stoop like
the neighbor's dog they had to put to sleep.

At poop time he will drag his leash from
the closet, jangling across the tile to my chair.
He will never get diarrhea and soil the Oriental
then whimper or cower in the corner.

And when I have my heart attack, I don't know
if he will punch 9-1-1 with his nose
like the schnauzer in the news,
but surely he'll cover my body with his so
the EMTs won't find me jittery with shock.

While waiting for the ambulance, I'll thank
my wife for this beast, warming the pain
a gift as perfect as our children who,
when we play tennis, won't serve as hard
as they can and will blow some shots
to let me think that by some necessary miracle
I've survived and will win in the end.

VISITING LORI AT SIBLEY HOSPITAL

The Jews call it a mitzvah,
Catholics a corporal work of mercy
for which the visitor earns actual grace
to deposit in his spiritual bank and,
at death, buy himself out of time
in purgatory (a place not as hot as hell
perhaps, we can't be sure, but hot enough
to singe you pure) while waiting for a spot
to open up behind the pearly gates.

Lori said after they finished
the carpentry on her hip, her blood
pressure dove several stories
and bottomed out at sea level
so they took away the Percocet
and let pain keep her alive.

Being alive makes it easier to laugh,
now, about the drugstore by the bed
her college students would envy, how
little blue pills make it possible, even
with metal hips, to golf on the moon.

One day I'll be dead and despite the pain
I've caused others, the selfishness
and breaking six Commandments,
embracing five deadly sins,
just because I shut off
the football game and drove to Sibley,
I'll burn less in purgatory, perhaps
a lot less because it was the fourth quarter,
the score tied. Perhaps a great deal less.
It was raining. There was traffic.

It doesn't seem fair
since Lori made me laugh.

JOY IN HEAVEN ON THE RETURN OF THE EGG THAT WAS LOST

While the pan sits on the old burner
and time softens the butter
as it softens all of us,
I tour the counter again,
pull out all four shelves from the fridge,
peek behind the fish, the tub
of grated cheese, the Kalamata olives
looking for the prodigal egg
that slept a moment ago
in the cardboard dormitory
with its brother.

Knowing an invisible egg
like a drowned corpse on the third day
will bubble to the surface grotesquely
announcing, *Here I am!*
I call the kitchen police.
She retraces my morning
from the newspaper on the blacktop
to the powder room where I never
misplaced an egg,
back to the stove, the garbage,
the sinister blades of the disposal—
all suspects now
in the glare of her terrible eye.

Then she jabs a finger in my gut:
*Didn't you put an egg
in the burgers last night?*

Are you like me? Searching
for something not there,
happy to find nothing lost?

LUNCHTIME APPARITION ON CONNECTICUT AVENUE

A double-breasted pin-stripe wears
a ratted-hair blonde wrapped
around his arm like a bulging pinky ring.
They are not close in age
but not illegal either and underneath
it all, she's pretty.

Her glance says, *Go ahead and look.*
or says, *Save Me!*
Catching my eye catching hers,
it's pinstripe who grins
knowing appreciation of an investment
inflates his stock. It's springtime
and a bull market on the bimbo exchange
so he'll hold his position a little longer.

Just as a rising Dow saved Clinton from Dole
this was a profitable lunch for all concerned.

THE STUTTERING ANESTHESIOLOGIST

His beard does not distract
nor his thick wild whiskers filter speech.
With much to convey, try to say:
"Propofol and lidocaine"
with your healthy voice.
He says, *Open wawide,*
wawawaggle the tatongue,
now dadadown,
testing for an open airway,
vital tunnel to the lungs.
Before the treasure hunter
snakes a hose up your butt,
syllables and sibilants multiply
faster than computers, and
is that his spittle sprinkling your gown?

Tell yourself a shower helps the harvest
whether peas or polyps. Tell yourself
one shitty day beats three years
of taunts he took in junior high.
He hovers close seeping night
into your veins. Forget
his complicated tongue.
Trust him to guard your sleep
and breathe for you while sharing
a fluent silence, his kind revenge.

THE NIGHT MY GLASSES FELL INTO A TOILET BOWL FILLED WITH CLEAN WATER

Even without them I could see
what happened. They slid from the tank
when brushed by my terrycloth towel
as if pushed off a cliff by a stiff wind.

Not handicapped by useless metal arms
we would have pulled ourselves out
or swum to shore and shaken it off
like any ordinary accident although
Freud said "there are no accidents"
which is something to consider.

But the glasses stayed under and still
as if content: two wet lenses
of slightly different talents like
fraternal twins, staring straight down
the drain, straining to discern some
dark secret from the old flow of family
life that we'd passed through.

The twins wait, like us, for the next
surprise, for a leap of faith to some
safe place, or just a helping hand
to fish them out, inspect for wounds,
rinse, pat dry, and send them back
to work, mute prophets looking
forward to focus a chaotic world
into images we think we understand.

/ II. OTHER MIRACLES

CROSSING EL RIO SAN PEDRO, PUEBLA, MEXICO

After two hours on a horse
Padre says if the water's too high
we'll turn back,
and the small Indian village
will miss Communion again.

The river proves hard to read
so he sends me first
on the shorter horse.

Current foams my ankles,
then rises to our flanks
and saddle bags.
Hooves wobble on rock
and a shock of river
flashes up my jeans.

Suddenly we lift off bottom,
pistons blurring beneath me.
He snorts froth as his muzzle dips
and dips beneath the surface.

We swim toward campesinos
waiting in a stone church
for what we bring,
waiting for what brought us:
release from the ground we know,
a ride through startling water
on the broad, slippery back
of an ordinary beast.

NOTE TO MY FATHER AS I NEAR THE AGE OF HIS DEATH

Remember that morning halfway
between the war you fought
and a war I fought against?

Dawn on Downey River:
you rowed, rowed into the mist
to leave behind our usual selves.

Yesterday disappeared
and we waited, imagining
what the water hid.

Then I hooked a lunker pike:
wild spray, thrash, leap, arc,
a lure locked on its lip.

You yelled, *PULL!*
But my line snapped, went limp,
the fish sank

and the river went back to sleep
while we, now wide awake,
re-rigged my gear.

When the sun melted the mist
we saw what we'd left on shore:
our ticking world, all its needs.

Back on land, our cooler light.
Three modest perch, enough
to prove we weren't skunked

but not enough to erase regret,
forget the silent ride home
or write a different poem.

Father, now I come one year short
of your death, and I remember
sitting by your hospice bed where

in a morphine fog you watched
the fishing channel as a Guide
made cast after perfect cast

to the right spot, and each time
he boated and weighed his bass,
I guessed which day you would die.

Death must be the last surprise,
a snapped line
closing the eye of the river.

HAUNTED

Now that we can't talk
or know what mattered most,
you are everywhere I go
or have been: in things,
other places, other times,

even in the tree you
stared at so long that
every color bled into other
seasons, and you swore you saw
your shadow in the wood

just as we saw subtle colors
blended in the clothes
you chose, frail fashionista,
before that final sleep in a pale,
thin gown you would have hated.

In '51 you and I threw pebbles
in a pond to watch as lips
of water rose to swallow stone,
and last week lips of flame
swallowed shrunken flesh.

I didn't know your death
would resurrect shades of all
the dead who ever loved us, so
I wouldn't be left alone, alive
with your weighty ghost.

GROSS ANATOMY: GEORGETOWN MINI-MEDICAL SCHOOL

The curious took a field trip
to the dissecting room; the squeamish
stayed in the lecture hall
or gave the line the slip.

Morgues hide in basements
windowless behind dark green
double doors. We breathe
refrigerated air and meet thirty
shy dead: one for every first year med.

Well-lit, generous cadavers gave
what last they had to give
to science, which was us. We watch
proud meds show off lungs pulled
like empty wrinkled wallets
from their brown and secret vaults.

The dead have kept their names
tagged in plastic but share the rest.
Look: here's a heart, a quiet fist
hidden in Ann Cole, her face masked
in a cloth bag for fear her cold stare
might resurrect her soul
and we forget she's just spare parts.

We won't forget the sour smell
alive in our street clothes,
why the meds wear scrubs
they leave behind while we carry
what we've learned back home.

WHY THE DYING NEED WILLS
Lawyers are priests who think matter outlives faith.

Clients, bald as monks,
eyes blazing, ride electric beds.
And bowls of wrinkled flowers
perfume the dreamy rim of heaven.

The cancer wing's gone thick
with green plants pumping
air back at their throats.

From the mirrors dangle
messages from missing children.

A nurse says one old salt swam out
from a coma and wrapped his hands
around a metal cross
as if clinging to a buoy.

A lifeguard in a lawyer suit
offers paper and pen,
a rope across the breakers,
pulling the past
toward new hands.

We want to give ourselves
away, piece by piece,
as if we owned everything
that matters.

So spring after spring we water
our sleepy grass and wait
for the children to remember.

WHILE VIEWING RENOIR'S LUNCHEON OF THE BOATING PARTY

The artist says the empty wine glass
is hardest to paint:
not just air but absence.

*What can I tell my friend
when he scatters his son's ashes?*

Elegant ghosts laugh on canvas
but the taste of the vintage
blooming in green bottles

by lush red grapes
eludes the brush like the shape
of the lost child.

*Where is the boat
that brought them here
as the fog waits for wind?*

TRANSPORT BY GPS

Closet the pinstripe life.
Unlock the bike,
its wheels so like the years
rolling round again
and back to the past.

That first Schwinn,
the battle for balance
each block further from home:
a fight for freedom
won once more.

Now it's time to leave
the woods of words
for woods, and clockless air
where clouds are more
than mist in magic sky

and trees more than trees,
gifts of shade hiding secrets
you will never learn
like a map you cannot read
or words in foreign tongues.

So you google GPS,
tap for maps, and
punch in "anywhere"
in hope a tiny lens in heaven
knows where on earth you are

or how you got so lost so long
while churning miles of time
on busy spinning wheels
with no advice to give
like where to turn, when to brake.

IN THE COUNTRY, DEER

Each night deer wander from the woods,
fan out, each to a different house,
a different window, waiting
for a woman to wake to their stare.

Once, from her bedroom Ann saw eyes
in the dark through bubbled glass,
a prism of rain, the sadness of two a.m.
Some say God watches every move.

Through the window of heaven He sees
our thoughts as if the skull were His theater,
knows the hour of the last breath
of every last soul until the end of time.

In the country is no theater, no zoo.
The walls of a cottage appear.
The deer watch Ann kneel by her bed.
Nostrils flare, ears twitch.

The deer wait for her to pray,
sing in her cage or flick a switch
to cover herself in a blanket of light.
Each night a new miracle.

WHY WORMS RISE TO RAIN

Maybe it's the steady beat above
like a distant heart
or just a silt-fed thirst.

So they twist and tunnel to sound
for a sliver of air
or moisture in coal-blind loam.

Are they deaf to a sentry of crows,
heads cocked, beaks ready,
stalking wet grass?

How long must they wait
eyeless in limbo
for the pulse of nature

pulling them closer
like all living things
to the mystery of light?

BLIND HAROLD

Follows a clickity stick, listing
to the left. Drawn to what's different
we stare at eyes flat as slate
and wait and wait

for him to blink in bright light
as we might
and maybe see him turn back
into someone just like us.

Perhaps when testing
darkness one may want
to wield some stick
as smart as his

to strike another way
(in spite of all the light
we lost) to wander
boundless ground.

ADVENT

As always it began
with an announcement
stunning us with joy in autumn

a time of disguised decay,
this season of invisible plague:
bodies ravaged, hope obscured.

But an unknown woman in white
studied the signs, a scatter of stars,
your young body, and said:

summon your shepherds, your kings,
your friendly beasts next April, then
lie down as earth awakes.

Now there's hope for a child
unlike a mysterious Jesus
we must imagine or invent.

We need what comes to remind us
of the humble miracle that brought us
from nowhere to begin our future.

So we await the promise
of a life that may mirror our past
and provide a prophet we can hold.

DISCOVERY OF THE NEW WORLD
(on the birth of a first grandchild)

Cristobal Colón imagining
a rich east, knew his roots,
risked the sea, trusted
fixed stars, a turning sun
and fresh wind to sail on hope.

Infant sailor, dream driven
fantasy, now loosed
in space, charmed by its arms
or a face at the edge of sight,
uncharted islands to explore.

We landlocked natives waited
on hope's shore to witness
first tastes of light and air,
ragged scream, harsh entry
to a planet of sound.

Colón bore gifts from an old world:
horse and pig, gun, germs and God,
changes for the earth, a path
to heaven, as if he were
the savior of a new land.

Infant, alien on land
like each of us, bearing
a virgin tongue—gifts
to be given, but like Colón's,
yet unknown and unimagined.

Born in New Orleans, raised in N.Y., **Gary Stein** graduated from Georgetown University and the University of Iowa Writer's Workshop. After earning his MFA, he spent six years teaching writing or literature in high schools as well as at Northern Virginia Community College and Trinity University in D.C. In 1977 he enrolled in law school and practiced law in the Washington, D.C. metropolitan area for many years. Despite a successful legal career his passion for writing persisted; he published numerous short stories before focusing full-time on poetry, starting with his first published poem in *Prairie Schooner* in 1974. He also co-edited the poetry anthology, *Cabin Fever* (The Word Works, 2004), and served for several years as Book Review Editor for *Poet Lore*. He lives with his wife in Silver Spring, Maryland where they raised two sons.

www.ingramcontent.com/pod-product-compliance
Lightning Source LLC
Chambersburg PA
CBHW022125090426
42743CB00008B/1015